MAMA TOOK CARE OF ME

—A TRUE STORY—

By

MARIETTA MURPHY

Illustrations by

JENNIFER HANSON

Illustrated by Jennifer Hanson

ISBN: 978-1-59298-604-0
Library of Congress Catalog Number: 2017901983
Printed in the United States of America
First Printing: 2017
21 20 19 18 17   5 4 3 2 1

Beaver's Pond Press, Inc.
7108 Ohms Lane
Edina, MN 55439–2129

(952) 829-8818
www.BeaversPondPress.com

To order, visit www.ItascaBooks.com or call 1-800-901-3480 ext. 118.
Reseller discounts available.

With special thanks to my family for all their visits and the help they gave Mama and me, and to Colleen Murphy Elsen for her assistance and support in writing this book.

CHAPTER 1

When I was little, Mama took care of me. I couldn't walk. I couldn't talk. I couldn't eat by myself. I couldn't blow my runny nose. I couldn't go potty by myself. I couldn't get dressed by myself. I couldn't even say my prayers.

Mama helped me learn to walk. When my legs were strong enough, Daddy balanced me standing up on his hand. "Oh! Be careful, Bernard," said Mama. "I think she's ready, Ethel," said Daddy.

6

Mama held my hands and helped me walk. *Step, step, step, plop.* "Try again, Mari," said Mama. "Good job." She helped me every day. Daddy did too, when he was home. Soon I could walk all by myself.

GOO GOO! MAMA! DADA!

Mama helped me learn to talk. I could say "goo, goo, goo." Mama said, "Say *daddy*. Say *mama*." I said, "Goo, goo, dada, mama." Daddy helped me, too. Soon, I could say *mama* and *daddy*. Then, after a while, I could say lots of words.

MAMA!

DADA!

GOO GOO!

Mama helped me learn to eat by myself. She fed
me with a baby cup and baby spoon. Sometimes
I blew bubbles in the cup. Sometimes I spit out
my food. "No, no, Mari," said Mama. When I was
ready, she helped me hold the cup. *Gulp, gulp.*
Then she helped me hold the spoon. "This will
make you big and strong." "Numm, numm," I said.
Soon I could eat all by myself.

Mama helped me learn to blow my nose. When I had a runny nose, Mama got a handkerchief and helped me. "Blow," said Mama. I tried to blow my nose. *Phbllbt honk.* "Good, Mari," said Mama. Soon I could do it myself, with my own handkerchief.

Mama helped me learn to go to the potty by myself. When I was a baby, if I needed to go potty, I just wet my diaper. When I was older, Mama said, "I think you are ready for the big potty." Every day she sat me on the potty for a while. I didn't like to sit there. I said, "No, Mama, no!" "But you're a big girl," said Mama. Soon I learned to go potty all by myself.

Mama helped me learn to get dressed by myself. At first, I got all mixed up. I got my dress on backwards. I got my shoes on the wrong feet. "Phooey!" I said. Mama helped me. She put my clothes on frontwards. She put my shoes on the right feet. "You look nice, honey," she said. I smiled. Soon I could get dressed all by myself.

Mama helped me say my prayers. We would kneel by my bed and say, "Good night dear Jesus, thank you for everything. Please bless Mama and Daddy and my big brother Darwin and my little sister Patty Ann and my grandmas and my grandpas on the farms and everybody in the whole world." Then she tucked me in and kissed me good-night. "Sleep tight, honey." Soon I could say my prayers all by myself.

CHAPTER 2

One winter day when I was five years old, I went with Mama, big brother Darwin, and little Patty Ann, to the corner grocery store in South Milwaukee. It was snowing and blowing. We got dressed in our snowsuits and boots. Mama pushed the big old buggy out the front door and down the snowy sidewalk. Little Patty Ann got to ride in the buggy. I wanted to ride, too, but Mama said, "No, Mari, you're a big girl now." "Oh phooey," I said. Darwin, who was eight years old, ran way ahead catching snowflakes. I walked beside the buggy. My bright red boots went *crunch, crunch, crunch* in the snow.

At the store, Mama picked up cereal, peanut butter, and some other things. She put them in the buggy on little Patty Ann's lap. Then we went to pay. Mama was taking the groceries out of the buggy and putting them on the counter. The store lady smiled at me. Then she said to Mama, "And someday, your little girl will take care of you." I was surprised! "Will I, Mama? Will I take care of you someday?" Mama was busy and didn't answer. "But will I Mama . . . will I?" "Never mind," said Mama. "Oh phooey."

We walked home in the snow. Darwin ran on ahead, catching the huge fluffy, puffy snowflakes. I walked quietly beside the buggy. My boots went *crunch, crunch, crunch.*

At home I waited to ask Daddy my question. When he finally came walking down the snowy sidewalk, I ran to the door. "Daddy, the store lady said someday I will take care of Mama. Will I, Daddy?" Daddy's eyes got very big. He took off his parka and boots. Then he set his lunch bucket on the kitchen table. He was quiet for a long minute. "But will I, Daddy, will I?" Finally he answered quietly, "Maybe . . . maybe someday you will." Mama was listening. "I will, Mama!" I said. "I will take care of you SOMEDAY!" Finally Mama smiled.

21

CHAPTER 3

In a few years, our family moved to Minnesota so Daddy could get a better job. Mama and Daddy had two more babies. Now Darwin, Patty Ann, and I were the big brother and big sisters. It was fun to have a baby brother Creighten and later a new baby sister Colleen. Mama and Daddy took good care of all of us. While Daddy was working at the machine shop, Mama worked at home.

On Mondays, she washed clothes and lots of diapers. Then she hung them on the clothesline in the backyard to dry.

On Tuesdays, she ironed the clothes and did sewing and mending.

On Wednesdays, she did some yard work and gardening. Sometimes she canned tomatoes, corn, pickles, and applesauce for the winter.

On Thursdays, Mama cleaned the house. Patty Ann and I helped by dusting, vacuuming, and shaking the rugs.

On Fridays, she pushed the empty buggy out the front door to the grocery store, the fruit and vegetable market, and the butcher shop. When she got home, the buggy was full of groceries.

On Saturday mornings, Mama baked bread, pies, dipsy doodles, cookies, and more. Daddy was home and worked outside in the yard and garage. Once, he made a desk for Darwin to do his schoolwork. Then in the evening, Mama and Daddy sometimes would get dressed up and go out dancing with friends.

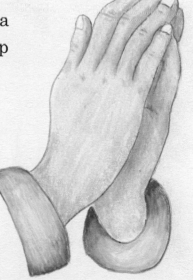

Sunday mornings, our whole family went to church. We thanked God for a good life and prayed for everybody in the whole world.

CHAPTER 4

The years passed by and our family grew older. All five children grew up and moved away. Most of us married and started our own families. A few years later Daddy died. Everyone was so very, very sad, especially Mama.

Then Mama lived alone. She was lonesome but she kept busy. She took care of her house and yard. She babysat for her grandchildren. She helped the ladies at church serve the funeral lunches. And, she often thought about her younger days. She remembered going dancing at the Ellsworth Dance Pavilion with Daddy, her brother Leo, and his wife Winnie, and other friends. They had so much fun!

In a few more years, Mama's grandchildren had grown up and Mama was old. Late one winter night, Mama stepped outside to get the newspaper. She pulled the door shut and it locked. She tried to get back inside, but she couldn't! It was dark and very cold. Mama was in her nightgown. She knocked on her neighbor's door, but Clara was sleeping upstairs and didn't hear her. Then Mama went to another neighbor's house. They also were sleeping. Lucky, their black lab heard Mama. He sniffed at the door. Then he started barking. The Clabos woke up and peeked out the window. They saw Mama shivering in the snow. Quickly they let her in and covered her with a blanket. Then they phoned Colleen, who lived nearby. She and her husband Curt got dressed quickly and went to take Mama home. Mama was safe, but now she could no longer live alone.

The next day, Mama asked me, "Will you take care of me?" "I will, Mama. I already said so! Remember?"

Soon there was a family meeting. Mama and all of her five children were there. "I can move back home with Mama," I said, "but, I'll need some help." There was a lot of talking and arguing. Finally, "We can all come and help," said Darwin, Patty Ann, Creighten, and Colleen. "You and Daddy took care of us, Mama," we said, "now we will take care of you."

CHAPTER 5

Then I moved back home with Mama. I said,
"Mama, SOMEDAY is here." Mama smiled,
remembering what I had said long ago.

Soon Colleen came to help on Mondays. "Hi, Mama, it's me, Colleen, your little baby girl. I cooked your dinner at my house. It's hot dish." Mama loved Colleen's good home cooking.

On Tuesday afternoons, Darwin came early. Mama was usually napping so he worked on his crossword puzzles. When Mama woke up, she was often a little confused. "It's me, Darwin, your big boy, are you ready for dinner?" Often she wasn't hungry. "It's okay, Mama, if you aren't hungry. How about some lemonade and peanuts instead?" Mama liked that.

GRR

On Wednesday afternoons when Creighten came, he didn't say hi—he put his bushy beard up close to Mama and said, "Grrr." Mama jumped and then she laughed. "It's me, Mama, your baby boy." He helped her to the bathroom. Then when she was finished, he said, "I brought you a cheeseburger, Mama, let's eat."

On Thursdays, I usually took Mama out for groceries. On nice weather days, we went to the park across the street for a wheelchair ride. Often we fed the birds. Sometimes, so many came quacking and tweeting we had to shoo them away. Mama said, "That's enough!"

Patty Ann worked late on Fridays, so her husband, Denny, and daughter, Liz, came earlier with dinner. "Hi, Grandma," they said, "we brought your dinner and a milkshake for dessert." When Patty Ann arrived later, she always said, "Hi, Mama, I'm staying overnight. Do you want your feet soaked?" Mama loved that. She splashed her feet in the washbasin.

On Saturdays or Sundays, I took Mama to church. We sang the hymns and prayed for everybody in the whole world.

Some days the grandchildren and others stopped by to help Mama. Her granddaughter, Kelli, came to cut and style her hair. "Do you want it spikey?" she would tease. When she was finished, she held up the mirror. Mama strained her eyes to see. She always liked her new hairdo.

Her son-in-law Denny, grandson Scott, and great-grandson Joey often cut the grass, raked the leaves, and shoveled the snow, as Mama had always done herself. Sometimes they asked, "Do you want to help us, Grandma?" She would laugh and watch them out the window. Occasionally her friends Rose and Trudy stopped by to help when I couldn't be there.

On holidays and her birthdays, all of the families came to help Mama celebrate. Darwin, Joan, Bart, Tyler, Carrie, Aaron, Patty Ann, Denny, Liz, Scott, Brian, Joey, Creighten, Jody, Kyle, Colleen, Curt, Kelli, Tim, Alex, and baby Shelby squeezed into the little house with Mama and me for brunch. She loved all the hubbub, especially when everyone sang happy birthday. Sometimes Mama sang, too.

CHAPTER 6

Now Mama is very old and I am in my sixties. Mama can't walk by herself anymore. If she tries, she might fall down. I say, "Now, I will help you, Mama." I walk behind Mama and hold her around the waist. *Step, step, step.* We go slowly. Mama tries her best. "Good job," I say.

When Mama tries to talk, she can't. She can only
say a few words. I help Mama talk. "Do you want
this chocolate cookie? Yes or no?" Sometimes
Mama can say "Cook . . . ie," or just nod her head.
I say, "It's okay. I understand you, Mama." She
takes a little bite.

When Mama tries to eat dinner, she drops her spoon. When she tries to drink out of her straw, sometimes she blows instead. "Oops, try again," I say and help her drink. *Gulp, gulp.* Sometimes she doesn't want to eat. I say, "This dinner is good for you, Mama. It will make you big and strong."

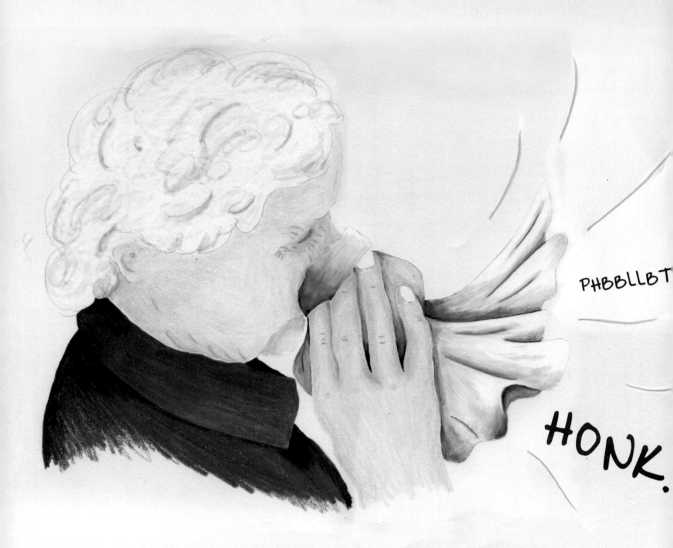

PHBBLLBT

HONK.

Sometimes Mama has a runny nose. She needs to use her tissue. "Uh-oh, Mama, here's your tissue. Blow." Mama tries to blow. *Phbbllbt honk.* "Good, honey," I say.

Mama can't get to the potty by herself. I walk her to the bathroom and help her there. Mama smiles. I think she wants to say, "Thank you."

Mama can't dress herself anymore. When she tries, she gets all tangled up. She gets her sweater on backwards. She can't put on her socks and shoes. "Phooey!" she says. I help Mama get dressed in the morning. I put her sweater on the right way. I put her socks and shoes on the right feet. Mama feels better. "You look nice, Mama," I say.

Now when I put Mama to bed, she doesn't say her prayers anymore! "I'll help you, Mama. Let's pray together. Good night, dear Jesus. Thank you for giving us a good life and thank you for everything. Please bless us and Darwin, Patty Ann, Creighten, Colleen, and all of their families, and please bless everybody in the whole world. Amen." I tuck her in and kiss her good-night. "Sleep tight, my honey Mama, and thank you for everything." Mama smiles a big smile and then she closes her eyes. Good night.

THE END

ABOUT THE AUTHOR

Marietta Murphy is a retired teacher from Minnesota. She works part time with special-needs adults. At the age of five, she told her mama that she would take care of her SOMEDAY, and many years later (with the help of her brothers and sisters), Mari did care for Mama in the same ways that Mama had cared for her. It prompted this true story, written for the family, but meant to be shared with other families, many of whom have their own similar stories.

Mari's parents, Ethel Cernohaus Kauphusman and Bernard Huppert Murphy, were raised on dairy farms in rural River Falls and Prescott, Wisconsin.

ABOUT THE ILLUSTRATOR

Jennifer Hanson came to the United States from Canada to study graphic design and run track at the University of Minnesota, and after meeting her husband, she decided to stay. They now live in Red Wing, Minnesota with their three children. A freelance illustrator, Jennifer loves to draw, finding inspiration in both her children and her beautiful surroundings. To see more of Jennifer's work, visit www.artworkbyjenniferhanson.com

A NOTE FROM MARIETTA

In writing this story, I often thought about how fortunate a child is to be raised in a loving family that provides good training and is not indulgent. Many children have no such support. Sometimes neighbors or friends offer to include those children in their own family outings. Many people volunteer to help with sports, scouts, and various other activities. This is a great contribution to those children and thus to society. We all know some of those people. We owe them our gratitude.